FINDING WHAT GOD HAS PLACED IN YOU!

Supernatural Relationships
With the Holy Spirit at the Center

OMAR C. DAVIS

Publisher's Note:

Spirit Led Publishing and Printing Group
Atlanta, Georgia

Copyright © 2020 by Omar C. Davis

All Rights Reserved. No part of this book may be reproduced or transmitted in any form or by any means, electronic or mechanical, including photocopying, recording, or by any information storage or retrieval system without the written permission of the author, except for the inclusion of brief quotations in a review.

ISBN - 978-1-7329054-9-8

Cover design, internal formatting & layout: Hemant Lal
www.AaronProductionsIndia.com

Contents

Biography	4
This book is about successful relationships	5
How it all started with me	7
My Passion	10
Becoming reborn	21
Lessons from Mr. Roddy Ripple	40
Spirit Wisdom	50
The New Chapter in my Life / New Creation	52

Biography

My name is Omar C Davis; I'm a resident of Savannah Georgia. I'm the father of two beautiful daughters. My passion is helping those in need, most importantly in need of Jesus Christ. I'm a member of Growing in Grace Ministry in Savannah Georgia. Fifteen years ago, God put it on my pastor Dr. Rodney Cutter's heart to start going to the inner-city night shelter every fourth Saturday to serve breakfast to the men and women that reside there. I started going and I started ministering before we served breakfast and it's been two years now. I also work with People Helping People and Matthew Gunn Outreach Ministry on Forsyth Park on Sundays, where they give away clothes, household goods, hygiene, and food. Jesus went to those in need! And that's what I'm passionate about!

THIS BOOK IS ABOUT SUCCESSFUL RELATIONSHIPS

NOTE: All scripture readings in the entire book are from The New King James Bible.

Most relationships are built on sex, finances, looks, emotions, intellect, and love for each other. These types of relationships are "natural."

Relationship: noun, the way in which two or more concepts objects or people are connected. On the state of being connected. Relation, link, correlation, alliance, interconnection, interrelationship, association.

Physical: (adjective) relating to the body as opposed to the mind. Physical leads to emotional.

Emotions: (plural noun) A natural instinctive state of mind deriving from one's circumstances, mood, or relationship with others (feeling, sentiment, instinct, intuition)

Material: Denoting or consisting of physical objects, rather than the mind or spirit. Physical, mundane, worldly, earthly, temporal, concrete, real.

This book shows what makes successful relationships and it starts with a personal relationship with Jesus Christ. This gives us a relationship with our Father God, which gives us a relationship with the Holy Spirit. This is spiritual! Supernatural!

It's life-altering for the good or the bad for the people you allow in your life. Think of all the people you have allowed in your life from the age of thirteen to twenty-five, thirty-five, fifty-five, from childhood until now. Many people are deceased because of relationships. Many are mentally disturbed because of relationships. Many are in prison for life because of relationships. Others are doctors – and all because of relationships. When you find the relationships that this book describes, your life will be taken to the next level. You will understand what successful relationships are.

We must use spiritual discernment to find these successful relations and the Holy Spirit is the center! Supernatural!

How it all started with me

Thirty years ago, at age fifteen, the year 1988 I walked into Burger King with Gary, one of my best friends. I go to the counter to order and I notice a girl…perfect face, perfect shape. Gary speaks to her. He knows her from the Frazier Homes where we live, and she used to live. Once we receive our food and sit down to eat, I asked him about her. I was seeking to find out more information about this girl because he seemed to know her quite well. He says things about her that are not too good but I'm not hearing anything he says because my attention is focused on the fact that I have to get with her. Before we leave the restaurant, I get her name and number. How that happened; I'm not sure because I was quiet and shy. When you grow up poor, you don't have nice clothes or live in decent housing, you try to stay low key. You never place yourself in situations that bring attention to yourself.

We started talking and I started visiting her at her apartment. I was getting dropped off to visit her daily. Over time I met her mom, dad, and older sister. Her father wasn't very talkative but I was always respectful to him. Shortly after we started dating her father committed suicide in their home.

It was nothing for me to go over to her apartment and just chill in the Livingroom for hours at a time. Besides, I wasn't much of a talker. I guess that's why we never really had a chance to get to know one another. Also, we were young and she was my first girlfriend. One day, I'm at her house and

Finding what God has placed in you!

a dude comes by to visit. She goes outside. At first, I don't think anything. I'm what most dudes from my hood would call "green" when it comes to chicks so I go outside. The dude is asking for his jacket that he left at her apartment. I'm standing there looking crazy because I didn't know anything about this dude or his jacket. I was really into her but after this incident, the "trust" was lightly damaged. I began to think about what my partner was saying when I asked him about her at Burger King during our first encounter.

Sitting in the Frazier Homes housing projects with my partners, like we did every day, selling rocks (crack cocaine). Out of nowhere the police pull up and block us in. They put all of us in the car, searching us for drugs but nobody had anything on them. The undercover police officer (Meadlock – who was later arrested for drug conspiracy and went to federal prison) says to me, "What's your name?" I respond to him by giving him my full name and he instructs another officer to cuff me. He stated, "He has a sale case". I'm thinking it's a joke but it's not because I get locked up. I was charged and sent up the road for a 4-6 month juvenile sentence. During this time away I don't hear from Jane; not one letter. She didn't go to my house to holla at my mom or anything. So now I have a really bad taste in my mouth for her. Although I was young, I still had the mentality that when I'm with you; I'm with you 100%. I consider that being real through thick or thin…I'm with you. Therefore, I expected that the people I considered friends would replicate the same mentality.

After serving my time, I came home with a bitter taste in my mouth for Jane. She failed to show her loyalty when I was away so I had an attitude about the situation. I started back hustling shortly after I got out. I didn't see Jane for several months and when we finally crossed paths we had nothing to say to each other. A year or so after we ran into one another, I heard she started dating a big drug dealer in town. She was 16 or 17 years old, in high school and he was about 24 or 25.

In my eyes, the girl that I once cared about was now a "gold-digging female"!

Many times, in our community relationships like this happen. It's cool because the dude has money and the girl lives in a single-parent household". This is like **statutory rape.**

My Passion

I didn't trust chicks after my experience with Jane, so I focused on getting money. My source of getting money was hustling. It was my primary focus. Thinking about chicks was second nature if I got with a chick it was for sex. During this time, the rap group NWA was popping. All they did was call women B's and this was the mental state I **adopted**. I say **adopted** because I chose to acquire this behavior based on the situation that transpired between Jane and me. When I was growing up, I did have examples of good or whole relationships. My uncles and their wives were together for a long time. I saw pictures of my uncle and his wife that were taken before I was born. So this was something I desired.

Gary, my partner whom I spoke about earlier we had a strong bond. I realized later in life the connection we had steamed from the fact that we were both serious about money. We met in middle school but when we became partners we would hustle together. When we would grind up $500-$1,000 he would go to the mall to buy clothes and shoes for school. After spending all his cash at the mall, he would come to me to hold $100-$150. I would give him the money, BAM no problem, he would turn it into $500-$1,000 quick. I would be like, I had to give my folks money for bills or I went and got fresh he would give me $100-$150, BAM, I would turn it into $500-$1000 and as we got older we would be there for each other. Whatever it was, that was our relationship. We continued like brothers.

Around the age of 18, Gary got locked up for selling weight (selling weight is large amounts of crack). He got caught in a dope house or (modern-day terminology) trap house and did two years in state prison. When it was time for him to come home things were different. I was stronger and wiser as it relates to money, and power in the dope game. I went to pick him up from state prison. Of course, I had all of the things that he loved...fresh clothes, shoes, and cash for his pockets. I remember him walking out of the prison doors. He was looking like "new money". I sat down with him and told him I didn't want him hustling. My words to him were, "just take it easy; I'm going to look out for you; don't touch nothing" because I didn't want to lose my brother again.

A couple of months went by and he took regard to what I had asked of him regarding not returning to the dope game. One day when we were talking he told me he appreciated everything but he had a son to take care of and it was time for him to get back in the game. I didn't want him to get back into the game but I had to respect his decision. Before long he was back into the game, doing his thing and winning.

At the age of 19 years old I lost my mother to her battle with alcoholism. Now I'm feeling a heavier obligation to watch over or take care of my brothers and sisters. It was six of us and my youngest sister was thirteen or fourteen.

A few months before the death of my mother I met a young lady. We started dating and I was serious about her about being in a relationship. She was a beautiful dark-skinned sister with a beautiful smile and pretty white teeth. She was the only female I ever introduced to my grandmother, so she was very special to me and my grandmother loved her. Two years later we had a daughter and by then we were living together. Things were good but personally, I was changing not for the good! During this time, one of my big homies was dating Jane's sister so from time to time he would tell me about Jane. He confirmed what the streets were saying about Jane dating the big drug dealer. I would see her in passing riding

Finding what God has placed in you!

in the dude's Mercedes Benz or something "flashy". At other times, sometimes within the same week, I would see Jane's dude come through Frazier Homes and pick up this other chick that lived directly in front of Jane's aunt's apartment. Ol' boy was cheating on Jane and she knew it.

Seeing Jane going to her aunt's apartment in the Benz I would be like "wow" to myself. She ended up having a daughter from the dude. A few years later the dude got killed. He put his hands on someone who came back later and shot him.

At this point, things were going pretty good for me until Gary/my brother was murdered. Me and my other partners really didn't know "why" or who did it, so I begin to carry an M-12 Uzi because I thought my life was in danger. On a cold winter night, me, Gary, and Ced were riding, drinking heavily, joking and the next morning I wake up to a call that Gary was dead. My partner who I love like a brother...DEAD. There's a lot of hate in the streets.

My partner's death took a toll on me, so I went up north to New Jersey with my family for a few months. This was an opportunity to escape the pain but not the hustle because my cousins were doing the same thing that I was doing down south in Savannah Georgia. Selling dope, drinking, and women; the average drug dealer's perfect trio. After spending time with my cousins, up north, I came back to Georgia with a business idea. I opened up an urban clothing store in the heart of the hood. It was cool because I got to go to Magic (clothing shows) in Las Vegas, Nevada, meet entertainers, and had fun all while introducing the hood to the latest and greatest in urban wear.

One day I was in my store and Jane walks in. I was shocked. She said she was looking for something. By this time, we are in our mid-twenties. She had gotten married to a 9 to 5 dude. I was surprised...no dope boy! She still looked good. There was a lot of confusion at home mainly because of my cheating. The criminal lifestyle changes a person for the worst. You not only hurt yourself; you hurt others around you. Jane told me she went to college and got a couple of degrees in education. She also had a child from the guy she married. I later found out her relationship with her first child father she ended because he was physically abusive.

I did that for about four years, still hustling on the low, mainly pounds of weed. I went from selling crack to weed to cocaine (coke). One day, I was in my place of business and 4 dudes walked in. They were dressed nicely but I didn't know any of the dudes. When they spoke I could tell by their accent they were from Atlanta so I asked them. They responded by confirming they were indeed from Atlanta and someone told them about the store. As I was about to show them some stuff all of them pulled out guns and pointed them at me and was like where do I keep the drugs. I told them somebody gave them the wrong information I don't sell drugs out of here so they took the money out of the cash register, my chain, a jacket tied my hands and feet with a cord and left.

After that incident, I decided to look into another business. I was too accessible, and I was tired of doing that. My new business venture was remodeling houses and building brand new homes, so I closed the store and started building houses. I partnered with this brother that had a construction crew. It was lovely seeing checks endorsed for $100,000 plus.

At this point in my life, I was good. I had a beautiful daughter who had the same mannerisms as me and she looked just like me. My daughter's mother took great care of my daughter and me. She worked every day then came home, made sure the house was clean and she cooked every day. Then eight years later we had another beautiful daughter. I still didn't get any better personally. It was always a side chick in my life. 2 or 3 years pass with a new side chick when I had an amazing woman in my life. I had eyes but I could not see. When you're the breadwinner you make things happen so no one can really tell you what to do. My life was about myself, my family, and my friends never seeing lack or poverty. I was passionate about nothing else but getting money legally or illegally.

Alcoholism ran in my family. I now understand it was a generational curse. My grandfather drank alcohol and most of his children including my mother were alcohol drinkers. Out of her 6 children, 4 of us drank alcohol. Alcohol was one of my vices. You make poor decisions when alcohol is a big part of your life. Now my nephew drinks, that's four generations bound by alcohol.

I heard in the street that Jane's husband was cheating on her with an old friend of hers. She found out but she forgave him. By this time, they had been married for several years. He sold her the "I will never do it again" and she brought it. She thought being involved with a 9 to 5 dude that would never occur.

There was a lot of confusion and arguing going on with me and my lady so I moved to my aunt's home for a while to get away from the arguing. My grandmother was very sick at this time. I had never seen the strongest woman I know and love so weak. She basically raised me. All the good in my life; I learned from her. She was loving and kind, the matriarch of my family. She had nine children she raised; my mother's six children and many others. She was my #1.

I remember thinking and saying that I wanted her to continue to live. If I could take her place I would because I wanted my children, my nieces, and nephews to experience that love that she gave me. She ended up getting worse and she ended up in hospice after a while. One late night, I was in the room and my aunt knocked on the door and told me my grandmother passed away. This was a day I dreaded my whole life. This is the woman I loved with all my heart. I didn't know what would occur to me if she had ever passed.

I drove my aunt to hospice. When we arrived at Hospice they informed us again of my grandmother's passing and gave us time to be with her. We called the rest of the family. My uncles came and my uncle who has always been the strongest, smartest (the one I always looked up to and emulated) I saw him with a frustrated, confused, and hurt look. He was and is the patriarch of our family. I didn't understand what was happening to me. I didn't crumble. I was very strong when my loving grandmother passed away. We all held hands and prayed around my grandmother's lifeless body.

Before the day of her funeral, I went and purchased a big sheet cake and a case of champagne. We were about to celebrate her life. I was grateful when she was alive. I did what I was supposed to do. I showered her with gifts and love so I had no reason to feel bad. What I didn't realize was that God gave me the strength. He was about to show and do some supernatural things in my life!

Things got back to normal. Honestly, it got better than normal. I ran into a plug and they didn't know how serious I was about getting money but they soon would find out. They were kind of paranoid at first, so I flew out to the border of Mexico to their ranch. Only 1 of the 2 main dudes (Migos) could speak English.

I went to talk about trees "mid", one of the top of the line types of weed, but what they showed me was "reggie" regular weed. I told them that would not work so he asked, "what about cocaine". I told him I could move it, but I wanted the mid. I know they had no intention of giving me weed. Cocaine is what they wanted to give me. I flew back home. They told me it was all good and we were going to work. They were going to get with me. I was thinking…yeah right, I wasted my money and time coming out here. About

Finding what God has placed in you!

a month later, I got a call from them and they sent some folks to Atlanta to meet me. During the meet up they showed me one block...a key of cocaine. They had another dude from Atlanta they had been doing business with so we came back to Savannah.

I moved the block of cocaine and sent them back on their way. Before they left I asked about the "mid". They said they were working on it. Shortly after, they came back with five blocks of cocaine. Street valued at a little over a hundred thousand and I didn't have to pay a quarter for it. By this time they were comfortable with me. We would talk while they were gone back to Texas or when they would be in Atlanta waiting on their other folks who I met later.

I would go to Atlanta sometimes to chill and wait for the work to come in. Me and the dude from Atlanta started talking. I found out he had another "plug" that was giving him a hundred blocks every three weeks to a month at like 18/19 thousand, bringing them to him and he screwed it up. He owed those people about 180 thousand. I was trying to figure out how you mess up 100 blocks when you sold all of them. Even if you only make $1,000 off each one that's $100,000 profit. I was thinking this dude is a clown and later I found out my thoughts were correct.

On the next trips, they brought 18-20 blocks. They realized I was serious about business and they didn't have to worry about me running off or coming short because there was no reason. Things were sweet. I had like three or four dudes that were buying all the work I was getting and my rule was I didn't care if they had someone else that wanted to buy some dope the answer was "NO". They also knew if they told someone they were buying the dope from me then they were getting cut off. You can't have everybody knowing you have work because the streets will start talking and the FEDS will start watching to see if what the streets are saying is true.

My Passion

Things were going great! The word on the street was that it was hard to find work. A drought came but Me and the dudes I was bubbling with were eating good. I pushed the price up to thirty-one thousand for a block. That was unheard of in 2007-2008. I built a 2800 sq. ft home on 3 acres of land I brought about 10 years prior, in the woods about 45 minutes to an hour outside of town. For some reason, I wasn't happy. I was getting money, drinking, going out of town to relax every weekend. My rules in the game were always straight up, if I'm with you…I'm with you, never steal or rob, be down with your folks to the end!!

Contrary to my rules/belief, everybody, I did business with crossed me, ran off with my money, or what I'm about to get into (I'm talking about my plugs) was the worse. I'm just getting back from Atlanta; my plug was in town with the work. I go to pick it up. We go to the secret compartment, transfer the work to the car I'm driving, I pull off. As I'm driving, I'm looking in my rearview mirror and I see a car following me. The car following me is a few cars behind me so I call my plug back. I asked them did they see a certain car following them and they were like man, you're just paranoid. I hang up; the car is still following me. I come up to an overpass so I make it through a light before the overpass but the car that's following me gets caught at the light so I make it over. I mash the gas and take a right turn into a neighborhood. I make another quick turn into an apartment complex and park. I sit there for about 20 minutes. I don't see the car anymore. I go to my spot, unload the 18 keys but I know that was the police.

I'm very paranoid now, not sure what's going on, so I start thinking. Every other week I get a new burner phone to work off of. Only a few people know I got work (cocaine). I also went and purchased a beeper (pager)and told my folks I did work with to page the number. They wanted to spend, and I would call to establish a meeting location. Little did I know it wasn't anything that I was doing wrong. it was the

Finding what God has placed in you!

clown from Atlanta that was slipping. After the next couple of trips, my plug called. The spot in Atlanta we had to move from because one of the vehicles they were moving the money in got stopped and searched but the compartment was so tight they couldn't find the money. After the incident, they decided to leave money from a couple of trips at the spot in Atlanta. Ol'Boy from Atlanta supposedly got caught on the road with a bunch of pills and cocaine. He got a bond, got out, and went to the spot in Atlanta and stole $900,000.

Only four of us knew about the house. I was in Savannah and the other two were in Texas. Everybody but him was at the house when we realized the money was gone. He finally called and said he took it. Anyway, not a dime was mine and he was their people. So we moved the spot to Savannah but we didn't know the people that ol' boy from Atlanta was doing business within South Carolina was working with the Feds and he met the plug and had gotten one of their numbers. He owned a club and they hung out so when ol' boy from Atlanta ran off they started messing with the dude from South Carolina, the one that was working for the Feds. But, I never went over to South Carolina or never met the dude. The last trip when they got to Savannah they called me. I went to meet them. Low and behold, I'm checking my rear and I see a car following me. The car is about two cars behind me. I pull over on the side of the road like something is wrong with my car. The undercover passes by me. I get back in my car, turn around, and then I take another route.

I get to the spot. I tell them what happened and they say I'm tripping so we load up, get in 2 different cars. They're driving the car with the work in it because they think I'm tripping. As we're driving, I see a truck following me, so I drive past the place we're supposed to meet thinking I could call my Migos and tell them to keep driving. The police are behind me! A car pulled in front of me and the back of me. I grab my chirp to try to tell the plug to leave the restaurant but the call would not go through. DEA jumped out with big AR-15 assault rifles, pulled me out of the car, and searched the car. They didn't find anything so they were looking like where are the drugs. They take me to the DEA building and they pulled up with the plug handcuffed in another car. The guy from South Carolina gave the DEA the plug cell phone number. They called the DEA in Texas and the Texas DEA started investigating the plug and was following them with tracking devices that they placed on the cars in the middle of the night. The device showed the vehicles going from Texas to Savannah. That day, at the age of 35, I didn't know my life was going to change forever.

I was charged with conspiracy to sell cocaine. The case was in Texas. Come to find out the DEA didn't know I was doing anything. The plug brought them to me unknowingly. They flew us from Savannah to Texas where the case was. Once I received the indictment papers and saw the United States of America vs. Omar Davis, I was thinking what have I got myself into. This was my first time getting locked up and facing time so I didn't really know what to look forward to.

About two to three months in because I didn't get a bond. It was denied. I started thinking about a conversation I had in the past with my Aunt Rosalee. I stopped by her house and she said, "sit down; what's going on?" We started talking We had serious talks about life often. I asked her, "What was it that made my grandmother so strong?" She lost her husband, her best friend (her husband's sister), her 5 sisters, 3 sons, and my mother. She worked in white peoples' homes, cooking, cleaning, and preparing their children for school when she should have been in school. She was 11 or 12 when she started working and that was the reason she could not read or write. I saw her at her son's funeral and everyone was crying, but when I looked at her in the front row, there were no tears. My aunt said, "Son, her faith in Jesus made her so strong."

Finding what God has placed in you!

    While I was in that cell I realized if accepting Jesus into my heart and being reconciled to the father got my grandmother through all of her trials and tribulations and all of her storms of life then He would get me through this storm that I got myself in to so I started to seeking him. **Romans 10:9** *That if thou shalt confess with thy mouth the LORD Jesus, and shalt believe in thine heart that God hath raised him from the dead, thou shalt be saved.* **James 4:8** *Draw nigh to God, and he will draw nigh to you. Cleanse your hands, ye sinners; and purify your hearts, ye double-minded.* I got a Bible that I could understand for a new believer in Jesus Christ. The KJV is kind of difficult to understand. I started reading and reading. It was amazing. I didn't realize or know it had all those awesome stories that capture your attention. All the promises for the believer.

Becoming reborn

I started attending church in jail. This faithful man of God, Mr. Roddy Ripple, came every Friday to teach the word of God and if he didn't make it, he would send Victory Magazine by Mr. Kenneth and Gloria Copeland, Jessie Duplintis, and Kenneth Haggins' magazines. I would read and underline and read and underline. I didn't realize I was renewing my mind with the word of God. Every federal facility I went to God had someone coming in teaching me the word of God. I would wake early in the morning while everyone else was asleep and watch Joyce Meyers and Charles Stanley. I would write down the scriptures they mentioned during their sermons and go read them and underline them. There was this Mexican brother named Julio Garza. He was a believer. He and I would be the only two inmates going to service and we would go faithfully. He knew the word of God more than I did. He and his wife were members of a church in Texas. He was facing life in federal prison. He was scheduled to go to court soon. This dude that was in the dorm with us asked Julio did he think God was going to stop him from getting a life sentence. He didn't respond. They took the things of God (praying, studying the word, going to church) for a joke. Like we were wasting our time.

I went to sleep, as usual, the night before Julio went to court. About 4 a.m. His will started replaying over and over in my dream. This is what I was hearing… His will. I woke up and it was still in my spirit. His will. I didn't understand what was going on. I had never experienced what was happening. I grabbed my Bible, looked in the back (concordance), and there was scripture and the page to find scriptures with His will. I read them and it was as though what to say was being given to me to share with Julio.

They told Julio to get dressed he was going to court. What was being given to me from God was for Julio. I told him when you get on the bus and someone asks you about his case; don't say anything. You're not going to get life; God's will is going to be done today in your life. I told him when you walk back in those doors, I want to see your hands raised in a show of victory. The situation was so powerful; nothing like that had ever happened. I didn't know what was happening. God was giving me all the words to tell Julio.

The whole day everyone was talking about what Julio was going to do and wondering what happened. About 4:30 PM Julio returned to the dorm with his head down. We were all looking awaiting to hear the verdict. The doors opened, he walked in and lifted his hands with tears coming down his face. **That day I witnessed the power of God manifest in Julio's life!** Julio's lawyer had told him to forget everything; there was nothing he could do. He insisted that Julio was going to be sentenced to life in federal prison.

From that day forth I knew God was REAL and his Word would not return void. Therefore, I will continue to seek God. **1 Corinthians 2:13-14** *When we tell you these things, we do not use words that come from human wisdom. Instead, we speak words given to us by the Spirit, using the Spirit's words to explain spiritual truths. But people who aren't spiritual can't receive these truths from God's Spirit. It all sounds foolish to them and they can't understand it, for only those who are spiritual can understand what the Spirit means.*

The only way to experience spiritual things is by receiving Jesus as Lord. **Romans 10:9-10** *If you openly declare that Jesus is Lord and believe in your heart that God raised him from the dead, you **will** be saved. For it is by believing in your heart that you are* *made right with God, and it is by openly declaring your faith that you are saved.*

And now you Gentiles have also heard the truth, the Good News that God saves you. And when you believed in Christ, he identified you as his own by giving you the Holy Spirit, whom he promised long ago.

John 16:13-15 *When the Spirit of truth comes, he will guide you into all truth. He will not speak on his own but will tell you what he has heard. He will tell you about the future. He will bring me glory by telling you whatever he receives from me. All that belongs to the Father is mine; this is why I said, 'The Spirit will tell you whatever he receives from me.* This is how "finding what God has placed in you" occurs. There must be a relationship with the individual and God!

I started trusting and depending on God my Heavenly Father, His son Jesus and his Word. He continued to show me His power. I begin remembering and applying the word of God to my life daily, the scriptures I was reading and studying. I started structuring my life around the Word of God. **Hebrews 4:12** *For the word of God is alive and powerful. It is sharper than the sharpest two-edged sword, cutting between soul and spirit, between joint and marrow. It exposes our innermost thoughts and desires.*

I received my time from the judge (96 months, 8 years), and a few months after I was transferred to federal prison where I would do my time. They had a chapel where worship service and Bible studies were held. To my amazement, they had guys in leadership roles (Inmates in charge of worship service and Bible studies). Inmates lead the worship service and Bible studies on Saturdays, but the chaplain would come in on Sundays. Black, white, Latino, corporate, drug dealers, embezzlers…you name it. Guys from all walks of life were there seeking and trying to grow in the things of God so when they received a second chance at life, they would do the right thing.

Brother Smith was one of the leaders. He would teach/preach 2 different sermons on Saturdays, one at 1:00 PM and one at 6:00 PM. They were always very powerful. I was told by one of the brothers in Christ that this brother couldn't read but when he received Jesus as Lord and was reconciled to the Father and received the Holy Spirit, God did great things through Brother Smith. Today he is co-pastor in a church in North Carolina.

We had three leaders (brothers) that led the congregation (inmates) so all would have to agree or disagree on an issue and when one of those brothers would go home they would pray and fast regarding the next brother that would become the new leader.

We encouraged, uplifted, and corrected when needed. We had preachers and teachers of the Word of God and we soaked it up like a sponge. In Bible studies, we studied the Bible book by book. **Proverbs 27:17** *As iron sharpens iron, so a friend sharpens a friend.* Because we all lived on the same compound, ate dinner in the same chow hall and some shared the same unit we knew if someone was playing or serious about the things of God. We knew where the brother in Christ was spiritually, so we held one another accountable and corrected each other in love when needed. **Ephesians 4:1-2** *Therefore I, a prisoner for serving the Lord, beg you to lead a life worthy of your calling, for you have been called by God. Always be humble and gentle. Be patient with each other, making allowance for each other's faults because of your love.*

I didn't realize until I reached this point in my writing. I thought back to the Bible studies on Thursdays when the Gideons of Augusta Georgia would come to the federal prison and teach Brothers Bill, Phil, Lou, and Musgrave. Brother Lou would be teaching, and I would be taking notes on the outline they would pass out and all of a sudden, I would start receiving from God. He (God) would start giving me extra information about what he was teaching. This happened often when Brother Lou taught. It would also happen when Brother Smith would preach/teach. These were examples of finding what God has placed in you. We were spiritually connected. What God gave the more spiritually mature or learned by the way of the Holy Spirit those of us who were less mature were learning and growing spiritually and finding our gifts, Glory to God!

1 Corinthians 2:10-13 *But it was to us that God revealed these things by His Spirit. For His Spirit searches out everything and shows us God's deep secrets. 1 No one can know a person's thoughts except that person's own spirit, and no one can know God's thoughts except God's own Spirit. And we have received God's Spirit (not the world's spirit), so we can know the wonderful things God has freely given us. 1When we tell you these things, we do not use words that come from human wisdom. Instead, we speak words given to us by the Spirit, using the Spirit's words to explain spiritual truths.* I didn't realize this until I started writing this book. This was an example of "finding what God has placed in you"! We were spiritually connected. What God gave the more spiritual or learned by way of the Holy Spirit those that were less mature were learning and growing spiritually... seeing the power of God manifest in each other's lives. Glory to God!

They (the leaders) would ask individually if we would do a word of encouragement that lasted like 10-15 minutes. We would do that 5-6 times then the leaders would ask us to do a word of inspiration. The word of inspiration would last 20 to 30 minutes (speaking time). We would do that 2-3 times. We would speak at the Saturday worship service both the 1:00 PM and 6:00 PM. The evening service would be full. Sometimes we would have to open the doors and brothers would sit outside by the door and listen to the Word of God.

Finding what God has placed in you!

When you're in prison it's painful to be away from your family. Not being there to provide, protect, and lead them as a father should. Some people run to cigarettes or hooch alcohol. Other men turn to homosexuality. The good thing in all of this is that some run to the Word of God. The brothers were seeing who had the gift of teaching or preaching and preparing us to speak in front of crowds and become leaders in our church because as years go by brothers go home. Time brought about change in leaders and the brothers wanted to ensure those who inherited the leadership were worthy.

Brother Nash saw that I had the gift of preaching. After service, he asked me to walk around the track with him. We talked about receiving from God and he gave me pointers. He pointed out one or two things that I should do when preaching the Word of God to people.

If we had not received Jesus Christ as Lord and was reconciled to the Father and indwelt with the Holy Spirit those things could not and would not have occurred. The Holy Spirit in us connected and we were edified, and God was Glorified. This can only occur in born again believers in Christ Jesus!

When the Holy Spirit in you is connected to another believer, you will grow spiritually. Your gift or gifts will manifest, and you and other believers will be edified, and God will be glorified. This is the way we build the Kingdom of God!

1 Corinthians 12:7 *Now to each one the manifestation of the Spirit is given for the common good.*

Glory to God!

All I did was study, read, listen to DVDs of pastors I had never heard of until 2008-2009. Pastor Tony Evans, Pastor Price…they had DVDs of Bishop T.D. Jakes when he had hair on his head. I took the Word of God and renewed my mind. For over 35 years I consumed a lot of trash which channeled the way I thought about things. I begin to fast every Friday to clear my mind as a means to create a gateway to receive from God. I stayed in my room, studied, and received a Word from God almost every time. It's a feeling that I had never felt... POWERFUL.

I had a brother that I was cool with in prison. He was my barber, Muslim in faith. I respected what he stood on (The Koran) and he respected what I stood on (The Holy Bible). We were talking one day and he explained that he was fasting for Ramadan. I noticed the Muslim brothers fasting year after year, so I asked him what happens when you fast for Ramadan. His reply was, "Nothing, it's just a Muslim declaration of faith. I proceeded and asked him, "Do you receive from your God" and his response was "no". Keep in mind I said I respect his religion which is different from me believing in his religion but I respect what he believes in. I don't believe in fighting and fussing about who serves the true God because time will tell.

1 Corinthians 2:14 *The person without the Spirit does not accept the things that come from the Spirit of God but considers them foolishness and cannot understand them because they are discerned only through the Spirit.* I give God all the praise, honor, and glory because he chose me. A foolish man, a man who was lost, a man who had eyes but could not see! And now because of what Jesus Christ did on Calvary; I am clothed in my right mind! Restored! There is a big difference between a man and a man of God. The Holy Spirit is what makes the big difference. The spirit of God is inside of the man of God and the man does not have it.

I believe the life of Paul truly shows us the supernatural power of the Holy Spirit! In the book of **Acts 9** when Saul is converted on the Damascus road, the Bible tells us he was still

Finding what God has placed in you!

breathing threats and murder against disciples of the Lord and asked letters from the synagogues of Damascus. That if he found any followers of the way (followers of Jesus Christ), men or women, he would bring them bound to Jerusalem. Suddenly a light shone around Saul/Paul from heaven. He falls to the ground. Jesus speaks to him, asks him a question. Saul/Paul asks who are you? Lord Jesus says I am Jesus, why are you persecuting me? Saul/Paul was trembling and astonished and said Lord, what do you want me to do? Jesus said to him arise and go into the city and you will be told what you must do. The Bible tells us the men who journeyed with Paul were speechless hearing a voice but seeing no one. Then Saul/Paul arose and when his eyes were opened, he saw no one. He was led into Damascus and he was three days without sight, and he didn't eat or drink. The Lord spoke to a disciple named Ananias in Damascus in a vision and told him to go to the street called Straight and inquire at the house of Judas for one called Saul of Tarsus, for behold, he is praying. And in a vision, he has seen a man named Ananias coming and putting his hand on him so that he might receive his sight. Then Ananias answered, "Lord I have heard from many about this man, how much harm he has done to your saints in Jerusalem. And here he has authority from the chief priest to bind all who call on your name," But the Lord said to him, "Go for he is a chosen vessel of Mine to bear My name before Gentiles, kings and the children of Israel. For I will show him how many things he must suffer for my name's sake." The Bible tells us Ananias went his way and entered the house and laying his hands on him he said, Brother Saul, it was the Lord Jesus who appeared to you on the road. Regain your sight and be filled with the Holy Spirit. Immediately there fell from his eyes something like scales and he received his sight at once and he arose and was baptized. The Bible says he received food, he was strengthened, then he spent some days with the disciples at Damascus. Immediately Saul/Paul preached the Christ in the synagogues that He is the Son of God.

Before Saul/Paul encountered Jesus Christ and was filled with the Holy Spirit, he was ignorant about the Holy Spirit. In **Acts 22:3** Paul speaking to the Jerusalem mob in the Hebrew language *I am indeed a Jew, born in Tarsus of Cilicia, but brought up in this city at the feet of Gamaliel taught according to the strictness of our fathers' law, and was zealous toward God as you all are today, I persecuted this way to the death binding and delivering into prisons both men and women.* But when the Holy Spirit enters Saul because of Jesus Christ his life changes forever. Saul becomes a wave of the power of the Holy Spirit in him and when that occurred Saul/Paul turned the world upside down. Before Paul/Saul could find what God placed in you he had to realize what God placed within you himself.

Let's go deeper in the Word of God, the Bible, and see more examples of **Finding What God has Placed in You**... Spiritual Connections, Supernatural Relationships. When this occurs, a spiritual gift or gifts manifest and the believer becomes confident in the word of God! The will of God and the things of God. We can look at the relationship between Paul and Timothy. Paul wrote eight to thirteen books of the New Testament. In **Acts 16** Paul is on his second missionary journey and he decides to take Timothy. **Acts 16:1-5** *Paul came to Derbe and then to Lystra, where a disciple named Timothy lived, whose mother was Jewish and a believer but whose father was a Greek. The believers at Lystra and Iconium spoke well of him. Paul wanted to take him along on the journey, so he circumcised him because of the Jews who lived in that area, for they all knew that his father was a Greek. As they traveled from town to town, they delivered the decisions reached by the apostles and elders in Jerusalem for the people to obey. So, the churches were strengthened in the faith and grew daily in numbers.*

Finding what God has placed in you!

Paul writes his first letter to Timothy and in 1 Timothy 1 Paul calls him a true son in the faith. The second letter Paul writes to Timothy; **2 Timothy 1:2** Paul calls Timothy a beloved son. Paul becomes Timothy's spiritual father. In **2 Timothy 1:5-7** *Paul says, I am reminded of your sincere faith, which first lived in your grandmother. Lois and your mother Eunice and, I am persuaded, now lives in you also. For this reason I remind you to fan into flame the gift of God, which is in you through the laying on of my hands.* For the Spirit God gave us does not make us timid but gives us power, love, and self-discipline. This clearly tells us these are two Men of God. The only way to become a man of God is to do what **Romans 10:9** says, *If you declare with your mouth, "Jesus is LORD," and believe in your heart that God raised him from the dead, you will be saved. Both Paul and Timothy have the spirit of God in them.*

And when there is a spiritual connection in a relationship, meaning one finds what God has placed in the other, those involved will be edified and God will be glorified. Merriam Webster's definition of **Edify** (v) 1. to instruct and improve especially in moral and religious knowledge: uplift: also enlighten, inform, build, establish. **Edified** – to instruct especially to encourage intellectual, moral, or spirited improvement (Glorify). Merriam-Webster glorified; glorifying 1. to make glorious by bestowing honor, praise, or admiration to elevate to celestial glory.

2 Timothy 3:10-11 Paul letter to Timothy *You, however, know all about my teaching, my way of life, my purpose, faith, patience, love, endurance, persecutions, sufferings—what kinds of things happened to me in Antioch, Iconium, and Lystra, the persecutions I endured. Yet the Lord rescued me from all of them.*

1Timothy 4:12-16 *Let no one despise you for your youth, but set the believers an example in speech, in conduct, in love, in faith, in purity. Until I come, devote yourself to the public reading of Scripture, to exhortation, to teaching. Do not neglect the gift you*

Becoming reborn

have, which was given you by prophecy when the council of elders laid their hands on you. Practice these things, immerse yourself in them, so that all may see your progress. Keep a close watch on yourself and on the teaching. Persist in this, for by so doing you will save both yourself and your hearers. When we read the letters Paul writes to Timothy he <u>instructs, encourages,</u> and in **Philippians 2:19-22** (Paul <u>commands</u> Timothy) *But I trust in the Lord Jesus to send Timothy to you shortly, that I also may be encouraged when I know your state. For I have no one like-minded, who will sincerely care for your state. For all seek their own, not the things which are of Christ Jesus. But you know his proven character, that as a son with his father he served with me in the gospel. Glory to God!*

This is not a book about relationships with just people but with people and God!

Glory to God! Paul poured all that God poured into him into Timothy! Why would Paul invest in Timothy the way he did? It's evident that the response is surely because **Paul found what God placed in Timothy! A spiritual connection!**

As I continue to give an understanding of what God has revealed let's go back into the Torah (Old Testament). Here we look at the relationship between Elijah and Elisha. This relationship is a totally different format than that of Paul and Timothy but the point we will conclude is that it is exactly the same!

Elijah and Elisha, also, two men of God (Prophets) in **1 Kings 17:1** *"Now Elijah the Tishbite, from Tishbe in Gilead, said to Ahab, "As the Lord, the God of Israel, lives, whom I serve, there will be neither dew nor rain in the next few years except at my word."* We point out some of the great and supernatural things that God does through his prophets. Elijah proclaims a drought, he prayed for drought and it didn't rain for 3 years, 6 months.

1 Kings 17:5-7 *So he went and did according to the word of the Lord, for he went and stayed by the Brook Cherith, which flows* *into the Jordan. The ravens brought him bread and meat in the morning, and bread and meat in the evening; and he drank from the brook. And it happened after a while that the brook dried up because there had been no rain in the land.* The Bible also tells us that God commanded ravens to feed Elijah at the Brook Cherith morning and evening after the water dried up. *Then the word of the Lord came to him, saying, "Arise, go to Zarephath, which belongs to Sidon, and dwell there. See, I have commanded a widow there to provide for you." God told Elijah to go to a widow which God commanded the widow to provide for him.* The Bible says she did according to the word of Elijah.

1 Kings 17:17-22 *Now it happened after these things that the son of the woman who owned the house became sick. And his sickness was so serious that there was no breath left in him. The widow's son became very sick and died. The widow asked Elijah (the man of God) "Have you come to me to bring my sin in remembrance and to kill my son?" Elijah took the boy's lifeless body to the upper room and cried out to God. The Lord heard the voice of Elijah and the boy was revived.*

The Lord tells Elijah to go to King Ahab and he will send rain. **1 Kings 18:1** *And it came to pass after many days that the word of the Lord came to Elijah, in the third year, saying, "Go, present yourself to Ahab, and I will send rain on the earth."* Elijah gives King Ahab a message. When the King sees Elijah he calls him O. troubler of Israel. Elijah says I have not troubled Israel, but you and your father's house have, in that you have forsaken the commandments of the Lord and have followed the Baals, Now go gather all of Israel to me on Mount Carmel, the four hundred and fifty prophets of Baal and the four hundred prophets of Asherah. Elijah said to all the people, "How long will you falter between two opinions?" If the Lord is God, follow him: but if Baal follows him. (Baal and Asherah false gods) the children of Israel were breaking laws of the Lord God) Elijah challenged the prophets of Baal to show that he served the only true all-powerful God

Becoming reborn

At the end of the challenge, the Lord God proved there was no God but him! **1 Kings 18:39** says *Now when all the people saw it, they fell on their faces; and they said, "The Lord, He is God! The Lord, He is God!"* **1 Kings 18:41** *Then Elijah said to Ahab, "Go up, eat and drink; for there is the sound of abundance of rain."* **1 Kings 19:1** *Jezebel sends hearts Elijah a spirit of fear overtook him, and the angel of the Lord visited him then the word of the Lord came to Elijah and said what are you are doing here. Elijah says how he has been very zealous for the Lord God of hosts, but the children of Israel have forsaken your covenant, torn down your altars, and killed your prophets with the sword. I alone am left, and they seek to take my life.* The Lord God tells Elijah to go to the Wilderness of Damascus and when you arrive, anoint Hazael as king over Syria. Also, anoint Jehu as King of Israel and Elisha you shall anoint as prophet in your place. (Anoint – to choose by or as if by <u>divine election</u>). Here is where Elisha comes into the picture. In the Torah, the Old Testament, only certain individuals received the Holy Spirit upon them to do the work of God. **Judges 3:10** *The Spirit of the LORD came on him so that he became Israel's judge and went to war. The LORD gave Cushan-Rishathaim king of Aram into the hands of Othniel, who overpowered him.* Also, the Holy Spirit could leave those that receive him. **1 Samuel 16:14** *Now the Spirit of the LORD had departed from Saul, and an evil spirit from the LORD tormented him.* This is the main character of this book, The Holy Spirit because he is the connection to the Lord our God.

John 14:16 *And I will ask the Father, and He will give you another advocate to help you and be with you forever-* (Helper names of the Holy Spirit). **John 14:17** (the Spirit of truth) *The world cannot accept him, because it neither sees him nor knows him. But you know him, for he lives with you and will be in you.*

Luke 1:35 *The angel answered, "The Holy Spirit will come on you, and the power of the Most High will overshadow you. So, the holy one to be born will be called the Son of God* (Power of the Highest). **Isaiah 11:2** (The Spirit of Council) *The Spirit of the*

Finding what God has placed in you!

LORD will rest on him- the Spirit of wisdom and of understanding, the Spirit of counsel and of might, the Spirit of the knowledge and fear of the LORD-; **Acts 5:9** (Spirit of the Lord) *Peter said to her, "How could you conspire to test the Spirit of the LORD? Listen! The feet of the men who buried your husband are at the door, and they will carry you out also."* **Romans 8:9** *You, however, are not in the realm of the flesh but are in the realm of the Spirit, if indeed the Spirit of God lives in you. And if anyone does not have the Spirit of Christ, they do not belong to Christ.*

1 Kings 19:19-20 *So Elijah went from there and found Elisha son of Shaphat. He was driving the twelve yokes of oxen, and he was driving the twelfth pair. Elijah went up to him and threw his cloak around him. And he left his oxen and ran after Elijah. And said, "Please let me kiss my father and mother and then I will follow you."*

Afterward, Elisha followed Elijah and became his servant, **1 Kings**. From the time Elisha follows Elijah God's power is being displayed threw King Ahab defeating the Syrians twice. Afterward, King Ahab makes a treaty with Ben-Hadad King of the Syrians and because King Ahab is disobedient to God, he was condemned **1 Kings 20:42** *one of the prophets says thus says The Lord. Because you have let slip out of your hand a man whom I appointed to utter destruction, therefore your life shall go for his life and your people for his people* **1 Kings 21:17-19**. The word of the Lord comes to Elijah. The Lord tells him to go to King Ahad (King of Israel) and tell him Thus says the Lord. *Have you murdered and taken possession? In the place where dogs licked the blood of Naboth dogs shall lick your blood. Elijah says I have found you because you have sold yourself to do evil in the sight of the Lord. Behold I will bring calamity on you. And Concerning Jezebel, the dogs shall eat whoever dies in the field.* **1 Kings 22:29-39** King Ahab goes into battle against King of Syria King Ben-Hadad whose life he spared and was told by the man of God to destroy. And in this battle, King Ahad dies. **1 Kings 22:35-38**. *The battle increased that day and the King was propped up in his chariot facing the Syrians and died in the evening. The blood ran*

Becoming reborn

out from the wound onto the floor of the chariot. Then as the sun was going down, a shout went throughout the army saying "Every man to his city and every man to his own country. So, the king died and was brought to Samaria. And they buried the king in Samaria. Then someone washed the chariot at a pool and the dogs licked up his blood according to the word of the Lord which he had spoken.

2 Kings: King Ahab's son Ahaziah is King of Israel now after King Ahab's death. **2 Kings 1:1-18** *Moab rebelled against Israel the death of Ahab Ahaziah fell through the lattice of his upper room in Samaria and injured; so, he sent messengers and said to them. "Go inquire of Baal-Zebub the god of Ekron whether I shall recover from this injury. But the angel of the Lord said to Elijah the Tisbite, arise go up to meet the messengers of the king of Samaria and say to them, 'I sit because there is no God in Israel that you are going to inquire of Baal-Zebub, the god of Ekron?. Now therefore thus says the Lord. You shall not come down from the bed to which you have gone up, but you shall surely die,' "So Elijah departed.5. And when the messengers returned to him, he said to them, "Why have you come back? So they said to him, "A man comes to meet us, and said to us Go return to the King who sent you, and say to him, "Thus says the Lord: It is because there is no God in Israel that you are sending to inquire of Baal-Zebub, the god of Ekron? Therefore, you shall not come down from the bed to which you have gone up, but you shall surely die." Then he said to them What kind of man was it who came up to meet you and told you these words? "They answered him, "A hairy man wearing a leather belt around his waist," And he said, "It is Elijah the Tishbite." Then the King sent to him a captain of fifty with his fifty men. So, he went up to him; and there he was sitting on the top of a hill. And he spoke to him, "Man of God the King has said, Come down! So Elijah answered and said to the captain of fifty if I am a man of God then let fire come down from heaven and consume you and your fifty men "And fire came down from heaven and consumed him and your fifty men. Then he sent to him another captain of fifty with his fifty men. And he answered and said to him. "Man of God, thus has the King said, "Come down quickly! "Elijah answered and said to them "If I am a*

Finding what God has placed in you!

man of God, let fire come down from heaven and consume you and your fifty men. "And fire came down from heaven and consumed him and his fifty. Again, he sent a third captain of fifty with his fifty men. And the third captain of fifty went up and came and fell on his knees before Elijah and pleaded with him and said to him. "Man of God, please let my life and the life of these fifty servants of yours be precious in your sight. Look fire has come down from heaven and burned up the first two captains of fifties with their fifties. But let my life now be precious in your sight. And the angel of the Lord said to Elijah, "Go down with him, do not be afraid of him. So, he arose and went down with him to the King. Then he said to him, thus says the Lord. Because you have sent messengers to inquire of Baal-Zebub the god of Ekron, is it because there is no God in Israel to inquire of his word? Therefore, you shall not come down from the bed to which you have gone up, but you shall surely die. So Ahaziah died according to the word of the Lord which Elijah had spoken.

Now ever since **1 Kings 19:19** When Elisha started following Elijah in **2 Kings 1:1-19** *Elisha saw all of those miraculous things that God did through Elijah and he probably heard of all of the miraculous things God did through Elijah, the man of God did before he went with him all of these miraculous things occurred because Elijah's God is omnipotent.* He has supreme power and has no limitations. The Omnipresence he is everywhere at the same time omniscient, God knows everything all-wise God! Glory to God! Then what occurred next clarifies even more. In **2 Kings 2:1-13** *And it came to pass when the Lord was about to take up Elijah into heaven by a whirlwind, that Elijah said to Elisha from Gilgal. Then Elijah said to Elisha, "Stay here, please for the Lord has sent me onto Bethel." But Elisha said, "As the Lord lives, I will not leave you! "So, they went down to Bethel. Now the sons of the prophets who were at Bethel came out to Elisha and said to him, "Do you know that the Lord will take away your master from over you today? "And he said, "Yes, I know, keep silent! "Then Elijah said to him, "Elisha, stay here, please, for the Lord has sent me on to Jericho. But he said, "As the Lord lives, and as your soul lives, I will not leave you! So, they came to Jericho. Now the sons*

Becoming reborn

of the prophets who were at Jericho came to Elisha and said to him, "Do you know that the Lord will take away your master from over you today? So, he answered, "Yes I know keep silent!" Then Elijah said to him, "Stay here, please, for the Lord has sent me on to the Jordan." But he said "As the Lord lives, and as your soul lives, I will not leave you! So, the two of them went on. And fifty men of the sons of the prophets went and stood facing them at a distance while the two of them stood by the Jordan. Now Elijah took his mantle, rolled it up, and struck the water, and it divided this way and that the two of them crossed over on the dry ground. And so it was when they had crossed over, that Elijah said to Elisha, "Ask! What may I do for you, before I am taken away from you? "(Now please listen to what Elisha says this makes it clear! Of the spiritual connection when you find what God has placed in you.) Elisha said please let a double portion of your spirit be upon me." So, he said, "You have asked a hard thing. Nevertheless, if you see me when I am taken from you, it shall be so for you: but if not, it shall not be so." Then it happened as they continued on and talked, that suddenly a chariot of fire appeared with horses of fire and separated the two of them and Elijah went up by a whirlwind into heaven. And Elisha saw it, and cried out My father, my father, the chariot of Israel and its horsemen! So, he saw him no more. And he took off his own clothes and tore them into pieces. He also took up the mantle of Elijah that had fallen from him.

When I look back on when Elijah meets Elisha and places his mantle on him, Elisha says "Please let me kiss my father and my mother, and then I will follow you." Later, Elisha cried out "My father, my father" when Elijah went up to heaven in a whirlwind. The first father was Elisha's biological father, but Elijah was Elisha's spiritual father because Elisha witnessed God do supernatural things through Elijah through the spirit of God being on Elijah. A spiritual connection occurred between Elijah and Elisha. Two men of God and Elisha grew in the power of God. After his relationship with Elijah, Elisha gifts were manifest and from **2 Kings Chapter 2 to 2 Kings Chapter 13** when Elisha died. Think about this: One person was raised from the dead by Elijah, the widow of Zarephath's son. But two people were raised from the dead by Elisha, the Shunamite's widow's son, and a dead man when he came in contact with the bones of Elisha after his death.

Imagine if a man and a woman who have both been born again believers find what God has placed in each other. These two believers are spiritually connected. They are friends both are growing spiritually together. They get married and have children. These parents continue in the things of God. Their children are 4 & 6. The parents start telling the children the story of how they both did what **Romans 10:1** says: how they meet each at Bible study or church, how they became friends praying for each other and fasting with each other when needed, how she was more spiritually mature than him but because they would discuss what the word of God said when it came to just about everything in their lives he started to mature spiritually and they were both excited about what God was doing they were being edified and God was being glorified. They tell their children all through their lives and show them by not fussing and fighting each other but praying and fasting about situations and casting these cares on the Lord. When those children turn 21 and 22 they know the story clearly because their parents told it to them all their lives so they truly understand the importance of their wives or husbands or boyfriends or girlfriend having received Jesus as Lord so they too can have the awesome experience of finding what 'only" God has placed in someone. **Proverbs 22:6** *Train up a child in the way he should go and when he is old, he will not depart from it.* This can change the generational curse of single-parent households if we teach our children this is how a dating relationship can be blessed. We have to find what God has placed in that person! In the US today nearly 13.6 million single parents are raising over 21 million (Wikipedia) children. The divorce rate in the U.S. is 53%.

63% of youth suicides are from a fatherless home (US Dept. of Health census) 90% of all children homeless and runaway children from fatherless homes. 85% of all children with behavioral disorders came from fatherless homes (Center for Disease Control) 80% of rapists with anger problems come from fatherless homes (Justice & Behavior, Vol 14, p403-26) 71% of all high school dropouts come from fatherless homes (National Principals Association Report) 75% of all adolescent patients in chemicals abuse centers come from fatherless homes. 71% of pregnant teenagers lack a father (US Dept. of Health and Human Services press release, Friday, March 26, 1999). **All of these generational curses can be broken if the relationship between a man and a woman is connected by the Holy Spirit and not by a person's looks, intellect, sex, or finances!**

Ecclesiastes 5:9-12 NKJV *Two are better than one because they have a good reward for their Labor. For if they fall, one will lift up his companion. But woe to him who is alone when he falls, for he has no one to help him up. Again, if two lie down together, they will keep warm, but how can one be warm alone? Though one may be overpowered by another, two can withstand him. And a threefold cord is not quickly broken.*

Threefold= three times as great or as numerous having three parts or elements.

Psalm 40:8 (Psalm of David) *I delight to do Your Will, O my God, and your law are within my heart.* **Hebrews 10:7** *Then I said, "Behold I have come in the volume of the book it is written of me-To do Your will, O God."* **1 Corinthians 11:3**. *But I want you to know that the head of every man is Christ is God.* At the point in David's life when he wrote Ps 40:8 and at the point of the writer of Heb. 10:7 if they would have met imagine how they would have edified each other and everyone around them and how God could be glorified. Two men or women or husband and wife that delight in the will of God and have the spirit of God in them.

LESSONS FROM MR. RODDY RIPPLE

Baptism in the Holy Spirit

Matt 3:11 ⎫ John the Baptist told his followers that Jesus
Luke 3:16 ⎭ would baptize them with the Holy Ghost

Acts 1:5 Jesus said he would baptize his followers with the Holy Spirit...

Luk 11:9-13 How much more will your... Father give the Holy Spirit to them that ask him?

Acts 1:8 You shall receive power after the Holy Ghost is come upon you

Acts 2:1-4 And they were all filled with the Holy Ghost

Acts 2:38-39 The promise is to you and to your children.

Acts 10:45 ...on the Gentiles... was poured out... the Holy Ghost

Acts 8:14-17 ...laid hands on them & they received the Holy Ghost

Acts 11:14-17 ...the Holy Ghost fell on them as on us...

Acts 19:1-6 Have you received the Holy Ghost since you believed Paul laid his hands on them and the spoke with tongues & prophesied ... about 12 men.

Mark 16:17 And these signs shall follow them that believe; In my name shall they cast out devils; they shall speak with new tongues ...

Lessons from Mr. Roddy Ripple

The Rapture (Catching Away)   Jail 4-18-09

(Jesus)

Acts 1:9-11   This same Jesus which is taken up from you...

Luke 24:50-51   ...while he blessed them, he was...carried into heaven

Mark 16:19   ...he was received into heaven & sat on the right hand...

(Saints of God)

I Thes 4:13-18   ...the dead in Christ shall rise first, then we...

I Cor 15:51-52   ...we shall be changed (transformed)

I John 3:2   When we see him we shall be like him...

II Kings 2:11   Elijah taken up
Rev 11:3-12   Two witnesses

The Second Coming (when Jesus comes back with his saints to establish rule & reign over the earth.)

Rev 1:7
I Thes. 3:13
I Thes. 2:19

Finding what God has placed in you!

Victory

5-15-09

All believers are subject to temptation. But victory can be yours if you use the resources available.

I Cor 10:13 There hath no temptation taken you but such as is common to man ...

I John 4:4 ... greater is he that is in you then he that is in the world.

I John 5:3 For this is the love of God, that we keep his commandments ...

Gal 5:16 ... Walk in the Spirit and you shall not fulfil the lust of the flesh.

Psm 119:11 Thy word have I hid in my heart, that I might not sin against thee.

II Cor 2:14 Now thanks be unto God which always causes us to triumph in Christ ...

Lessons from Mr. Roddy Ripple

Rewards
5-22-09

Heb 11:6 ...he is a rewarder of them that seek him

Heb 10:35 Cast not away your confidence...great Reward.
(See I John 5:14-15)

Heb 11:24-26 Moses had respect to the payment of the Reward

I Cor 3:8 ...man shall receive...reward according to his labor.

Matt 6:4 Father which sees in secret shall reward you openly.

Matt 5:12 Rejoice...for great is your Reward in heaven

Luke 6:35 ...do good...and your Reward shall be great

Psm 19:7-11 Gods laws are perfect...in keeping them is great Reward.

Rev 22:12 ...I come quickly, and my Reward is with me

Finding what God has placed in you!

Nothing To Fear

5-29-09

II Tim 1:7 — For God has not given us a spirit of fear...

Matt 14:25-31 (Fear is the opposite of faith)
...when he saw the wind, he was afraid.. (*for 4:7)

Matt 25:24-25 — And I was afraid & hid your money in the earth

Luke 21:26 — Men's hearts failing them for fear...

Rev 21:8 — But the fearful and unbelieving shall have their part in the lake of fire

---

Gen 26:24 — Fear not, I am with thee

Ish 41:10 — Fear not, I am with thee

Ish 43:1-2 — Fear not, I have redeemed thee

Psm 118:6 — The Lord is on my side; I will not fear
(God is on my side; I am on God's side.)

I John 4:18 — There is no fear in love; but perfect love casts out fear.

Lessons from Mr. Roddy Ripple

— The Church — 6-5-09

Col 1:18 And he is the head of the body, the church... I Cor 12:11

Acts 2:42 ... they continued —
    ① in the apostles doctrine   II Tim 3:16
    ② in fellowship   Heb 10:25
    ③ in breaking of bread   I Cor 11:29-34
    ④ in prayers   I Cor 14:26, Acts 4:30-31

Matt 18:20   For where two or three are gathered in my name...

Gal 6:2   Bear one anothers burdens ...

Heb 10:25   Forsake not the assembling of yourselves together...

John 13:34-35   ...love one another

Gal 6:9-10   ...do good, especially to ... the household of faith.

Eph 4:11-13   And he gave apostles, prophets, evangelists, pastors and teachers; for the perfecting of the saints, for the work of the ministry, for the edifying (building up) of the body of Christ.

Receiving Holy Spirit:
Mat 3:11   Jn 7:37
Luke 3:16   Acts 19:6
Acts 1:4   Acts 2:39
Mark 16:17
Acts 1:8
   2:4
   11:15-17
   10:45-47

Finding what God has placed in you!

The Mote and the Beam 6-19-09

Matt 7:1-5 — ① Judge not that you be not judged.
② Why do you look at the speck (mote) in your brother's eye and do not see the beam (budding material) in your own eye?

John 8:3-11 — Woman taken in adultry. Neither do I accuse you.

Rev 12:10 — The accuser of our brethern is cast down...

Job 2:1-6 — Satan, have you considered my servant Job?

Rom 12:17-19 — Vengence is mine...says the Lord.

Duet 32:35 — To me belongs vengence

I Sam 25:2- — David, Nabal + Abigail

Prov 26:27 — Whoso digs a pit shall fall therein...

Matt 5:44 — Love your enemies, bless them that curse you...

ISAIAH 61:1

Lessons from Mr. Roddy Ripple

6-26-09

Matt 19:24 It is easier for a camel to go thru the eye of a needle, than for a rich man to enter the Kingdom of God.

Matt 20:1-16 Laborers in the Vineyard (Talents Matt 25:20)

Matt 22:23-30 Whose wife will she be in heaven?

Acts 13:33 Jesus was "begotten" when he was raised from the dead. See John 3:16 & 17

John 6:37-40 ...will of God - that all Father has given Me (Jesus) I lose nothing. (No one is able to snatch - Jn 10:29)

I Cor 6:15-20 ... your body is the temple of the Holy Spirit & you are not your own.

Finding what God has placed in you!

The Church   Jail 7-24-09

Matt 18:20   Where two or three are gathered together...
I Cor 11:3   ... head of every man is Christ... head of Christ is
Col 1:18   ... he is the head of the body, the church ...
Eph 5:23   Christ is the head of the church ...
   22-25

Acts 2:42 ... devoted themselves to the Apostles teaching ...

Eph 4:11-13 ... gave some to be apostles, some prophets ...

Heb 10:25 ... forsake not the assembling of ourselves ...

John 13:34-35 A new commandment I give you

Galations 6:2 Carry each others burdens ...

I Cor 13:4-8   Charity (love)

Lessons from Mr. Roddy Ripple

Jail 10-2-09

<u>Sin</u> Offering
Lev 4:27-31   common people s. u thru ignorance

Mark 12:28-33 ...to love God ;: more than burnt offerings
Mark 9:1 ...shall not taste ... th till... Kingdom of God come

Take up your <u>cross</u>
Mark 8:34-38

Mark 10:17-31

Spirit Wisdom

Before we go further let's look at two scriptures that speak to the significance of the Holy Spirit.

1 Corinthians 2: *And I, brethren, when I came to you did not come with excellence of speech or of wisdom declaring to you the testimony of God. For I determined not to know anything among you except Jesus Christ and him crucified. I was with you in weakness, in fear, and in much trembling. And my speech and my preaching were not with persuasive words of human wisdom, but in demonstration of the Spirit and of power. That your faith should not be in the wisdom of men but in the power of God. However, we speak wisdom among those who are mature, yet not the wisdom of this age, nor of the rulers of this age, who are coming to nothing, But we speak the wisdom of God in a mystery, the hidden wisdom which God ordained before the ages for our glory. Which none of the rulers of this age knew, for had they known, they would not have crucified the Lord of Glory. But as it is written," Eye has not seen, nor ear heard nor have entered into the heart of man the things which God has prepared for those love him". But God has revealed them to us through His Spirit, for the Spirit searches all things yes, the deep things of God. For what man knows the things of a man except for the spirit of the man which is in him? Even so, no one knows the things of God except the Spirit of God. Now we have received, not the spirit of the world, but the Spirit who is from God that we might know the things that have been freely given to us by God.*

2 Peter 1:21 for prophecy never came by the will of man, but holy men of God spoke as they were moved by the Holy Spirit.

When we look at what's called out in these two scriptures, we see clearly why the Holy Spirit must be present in our relationships!

The New Chapter in my Life / New Creation

I was really looking forward to going home. My goal was to try and right my wrongs with my children's mother. Time was getting close for me now. I was waiting on my out date the date I would be going to the halfway house. I was mentally and, most importantly, spiritually prepared. A new creation in Christ Jesus but the real test would come when I got back to the streets, my family thought. My mind was made up. I would not be like a dog returning to his vomit. I knew people would be doing the same things they were doing when I left the streets: freaking, getting high, and chasing money or I should say chasing the wind. I used that time in federal prison wisely!

The day came and my family was coming to pick me up from federal prison. That morning I got dressed and was ready to hear them call my name. At about 8:30, they called my name. I grabbed my bags and headed out. I spoke to some brothers on the way out. It was great walking out of the prison doors and getting in the car with my family. We talked, stopped, and got something to eat. I couldn't stop smiling at my girls and their mom. We made it to Savannah, and I had a couple of hrs., so we stopped by our home. it was my first time seeing the home because my kid's mother purchased the home while I was incarcerated. It was a beautiful home. 4br, 3 baths, and a huge yard. I went into a room and got some clothes to take to the halfway house and we left for the halfway house. Federal prison was a mental institution and the halfway house was just a smaller version. it was a nuthouse. People up all night talking when we had to get up at 5 am

The New Chapter in my Life / New Creation

for work. I'm in the restroom trying to shower and they are smoking cigarettes like it's legal to come out the shower your clothes smelling like smoke, the crazy thing is you have to get used to it because they would not stop. One Saturday, I received a pass to go to Walmart, so I stopped to get some gas and as I was pumping I heard someone call my name I turned around it was Jane and her older sister. I walked over hugged them and told them they looked good and asked about their families before I left, they invited me to their church. I hadn't seen Jane in 10 to 15 years. I saw her older sister about 6 or 7 years ago but I talked to her a couple of times when I was incarcerated. I called to speak or check on her husband. One time I called Jane was there her sister put her on the phone, I asked how was her family? I told her it was good to hear her family was well. I stayed in the halfway house for about a month and they sent me on home confinement. Now I could build a sure foundation under our relationship Jesus Christ.

Before I left the halfway house, I was searching for a church home. I went to two or three different churches, but they didn't feel right when I went to home confinement, someone invited my children's mother to this church we went together, and we really enjoyed it. She had a church home, but the pastor was indicted by the feds, and she and my girls stopped going. I would go to this church by myself at times and I really enjoyed it. They had young men and women that loved the Lord and the pastor preached powerful sermons. I started going week after week and the messages continued to be powerful. I realized this was the church home for me, not to mention they had an outreach ministry that went to the homeless shelter every 4th Saturday feeding the homeless and giving them clothes. I said the church I became a member of had to go to those in need of material things but most important in need of the Savior of the world (Jesus Christ). One Sunday as I was leaving service I saw Jane & Karen her sister, and they were just as surprised as I was. Karen and I walked towards our vehicles. I asked about her family and

Finding what God has placed in you!

she asked about mine. I told her. I talked to her husband a few days ago. We talked for a minute as she waited for Jane. We talked about growing spiritually, how the things of the world didn't hold as much value as it once did in her life. I was like Praise God! When you have lived a life of chasing the things of the world (the wind) you will never catch it or be satisfied if you did catch it. I was truly happy to hear that. I love to see someone that was blind but now they see. Only our Father who art in heaven can do this. By a person receiving His Son Jesus! She asked about my children's mother. I told her she was fine I have been trying to right my wrongs of the past and make the foundation of our relationship Jesus Christ but when a person doesn't understand spiritual warfare and the weapons that the believers have to use. The enemy will cause havoc in your relationship. She told me how her sister (Jane) was going through it with her husband also. I hugged her and told her I would see her later and I would keep them in my prayers. She went back to the church to get Jane.

Before all the confusion started at home, I talked to my children's mother about us getting married, I wanted to do things right by her and most importantly God. So, we talked about it. She wanted a wedding but I just came home and I explained you can have a million-dollar wedding or go to the courthouse but it has to be built on the solid rock Jesus Christ for it to be blessed. Before I was incarcerated we had been together 17 yrs. marriage wasn't important to me and I didn't understand the importance of marriage. So we went to the courthouse, signed the papers but we decided to go in front of a pastor. But things started going downhill fast. She was expecting things from me and I expected things from her and neither was getting it, I guess divide and conquer started to occur, we were in disagreements more than agreements. The Bible says how can two work together unless there is agreement. We stop going to church together, I decided I was going to move and we weren't going to get married again. But I continued to pray for her, and I believe she's praying

The New Chapter in my Life / New Creation

for me. I continued to focus on work and staying on the path of righteousness for His namesake. One Sunday I was going to service and as I parked my car, I saw Jane and as she and I were walking she told me her mother had a light stroke and she was in the hospital and her mom is a very sweet lady, so I asked how could I get in contact with her mother to check on her. She gave me her phone number and told me to text her and she would text me the information regarding her mother. In a day or so I texted her and got her mother's information. I called her and spoke with her just letting her know that I would be praying for her and I was just making sure she was ok. I texted Jane to let her know I spoke with her mother and I gave her some scriptures to read regarding God's promises about healing and strength in time of weakness. She was surprised and thankful, so I told her Glory to God. As a child of the Most High the true and living God all we have is His word to trust and believe regarding everything that occurs in our lives, good or bad. And she was very receptive and very grateful. Jane had never heard me speak the word of God and this puzzled her and intrigued her at the same time because all she remembers was when I was in the streets and know I am articulating the Word. And I felt the same way she was saying Amen and speaking the word also, but I understand that nothing is too hard for the God we serve. In my mind, I was giving God glory because it seemed like God was doing a work in her life. Any time you see someone that was lost and has been found by God that is a great thing. The curiosity to find out more about the change that has occurred began to drive our future conversations, the calls between Jane and I went from short occasional talks to frequent comforting conversation fairly quickly due to the like-mindedness. We even shared similar values and views. A situation came up with Jane's job and she was thinking about transferring, she mentioned it to me saying she really wanted the job so I told her let's fast regarding you getting the job, so I found scriptures regarding Him Supplying all of our needs **Ephesians 3:20.**

Finding what God has placed in you!

God can do exceeding abundantly above all that we ask or think. How he is our Jehovah Jireh My Provider, **Matthew 7:11**. If you then who are evil know how to give good gifts to your children, how much more will your Father in heaven give good things to those who ask?

We finished the fast and shortly after she received the job. She was amazed at how fast God answered. And we just gave Him Glory over the phone. I pointed out that scripture tells us that if two of you agree here on earth concerning anything you ask, my father in heaven will do it for you. And that's how our spiritual friendship relationship started. It was about praying for our families and trying to grow spiritually having God show up in our lives and our family lives. There was a situation where I was trying to get this job, there were some credentials that I needed and it's hard to get and takes a long time to get when you are a convicted felon but nothing is too hard for the God whom we serve. When Jesus died on Calvary and was raised from the dead with all power and we received him as Lord our sins were forgiven and erased. Jane agreed with me, we prayed over the phone and it took some time but I received the credentials for that job and sometime later we prayed and thanked God for His favor regarding me getting off federal probation early, the probation officer said it was too soon give it another year, year and a half. I got those credentials, I received character letters and I wrote a letter telling them why I believe I no longer needed to be on federal probation. Shortly after that, the probation officer texted me and said she had some good news for me. I went there to her office she said that my probation was terminated but I couldn't get arrested I told her I work, go home, and church. I couldn't get arrested for any of those.

This is what occurs when you find what God has placed in someone. There's a building up (edifying). The person grows spiritually. They see the other person or people of faith and how they walk by faith and talk by faith. How the power of

The New Chapter in my Life / New Creation

God manifests in the life of the person and how because there's a spiritual connection. This is a gift from God to those that find it and how great it is. To receive this gift those involved must be born again (born from above) the need for spiritual transformation or regeneration produced by the Holy Spirit. Glory to God! This book came to life because God, Holy Spirit then the friendship/relationship that Jane and I had or have and most important the Holy Spirit in her and myself when God revealed the name to me finding what God has placed in you and I started thinking of examples in the Bible. My first thoughts were a male and female friendship/relationship Aquila and his wife Priscilla but their spiritual development relation was not shown enough in the scripture (spiritual development). But Paul and Timothy would be perfect and so would Elijah & Elisha and I saved Jane and myself for last. If it lines up then God will be glorified and the body would be edified three different scenarios about spiritual friendships/relationship and spiritual connections but in all of them, it's about the Holy Spirit and how spiritual development occurs in those involved lives. These relationships are about the spirit, not the flesh and this is what is missing in relationships today. The center of a relationship/friendship must be God! I was lying in bed on June 19, 2017, watching TBN the Christian TV channel (Trinity Broadcasting Network) which I do often looking to hear a word from God from the Preachers Teachers of Gospel of Jesus Christ and it said up next on praise Mr. TD Jakes his wife Mrs. Serita Jakes, Mr. John Gray, Mrs. Sheryl Brady and Mr. Tye Tribbett and music by Grace I thought I'm about to watch this as I thought it was blessing me personally and then what Mr. TD Jakes and Mrs. Serita said made me start thinking. This is finding what God has placed in you.

I wrote the date down and everyone that was on the show down because this is what occurs in a marriage when both parties are believers. Glory to God! Mr. TD Jakes starts by saying his wife was an introvert. She was shy and they never had to fight over the microphone because she didn't want to

Finding what God has placed in you!

talk to people, Mr. TD Jakes said. But there were gifts inside of her and he told her that when she didn't see it in herself. He told her who she was. He talked about husbands believing in their wives. He helped her find who she was in Christ! He edified her and because of that God is being glorified. He found what God placed in her and a spiritual connection occurred. She grew spiritually and now she speaks to the people of God with boldness and authority not because who she is but because of who our God is and her having the Holy Spirit in her the spirit of God! Imagine if marriages were built on the spirit of God, the word of God, and how good it feels when both parties love God and live their lives trying to honor God, getting their direction from the Holy Spirit! Glory to God! He has blessed us with a gift that money can't buy. The only way to receive this gift is to accept Jesus Christ as Lord **Romans 10:9-10** of your life! When I think about it the Holy Spirit in all five of these people of God on TBN connected spiritually that night in the studio was edified. The people watching on TV were edified and the God we serve was glorified. That was not scripted. That was the work of the Holy Spirit! I thank God for TBN Trinity Broadcasting Network spreading the gospel! Please get a full understanding. Go to TBN (Praise) and watch it when Mr. TD Jakes starts to talk about his wife, she speaks about him! When you go to TBN and pull the clip up, it starts for 17 minutes and 42 seconds into the clip. Please watch and listen.

When a follower of Christ, a Believer, gets in a relationship with an unbeliever you cannot find what God has placed in them because it is not there. When we look back into the (Old Testament) **1 Kings 3:5-14** *The Lord appeared to Solomon in a dream by night and God said Ask! What shall I give you? Solomon said, "You have shown great mercy to your servant David my father, because he walked before you in truth, in righteousness and unrighteousness of heart with you, you have continued this great kindness for him and you have given him a son to sit on his throne, as it is this day. Now, O Lord my God, you have made your Servant*

King instead of my father David, but I am a little child. I do not know how to go out or come in. And Your Servant is in the midst of your people whom you have chosen, a great people, too numerous to number or count. Therefore, give to Your Servant an understanding heart to judge your people that I may discern between good and evil. The speech pleased the Lord, that Solomon had asked this thing. Then God said to him because you asked this thing and have not asked riches for yourself, nor have asked the life of your enemies but have asked for yourself understanding and to discern justice. Behold I have done according to your words, I have given you a wise and understanding heart so that there has not been anyone like you before you nor shall any like you arise after you. And I have also given you what you have not asked both riches and honor so that there shall not be anyone like you among the kings all your days. So, if you walk in my ways to keep my statutes and my commandments as your father David walked, then I will lengthen your days. A two-way conversation with God and Solomon, so God was with King Solomon that's clear.

Now when we look back in **Deuteronomy 6**, Moses gives statutes and judgments which the Lord God has commanded. **Deuteronomy 6:14-15** *You shall not go after other gods, the Gods of the peoples who are all around you is for the Lord your God is a jealous God among you lest the anger of the Lord your God be aroused against you and destroy you form the face of the earth.* **Deuteronomy 7:26** *you shall make no covenant with them nor make marriages with them; you shall not give your daughters to their sons nor take their daughter for your son. For they will turn your sons away from following Me, to serve other gods; so, the anger of the Lord will be aroused against you and destroy you suddenly.* But we see what occurs with King Solomon in **1 Kings 11:1** *But King Solomon loved many foreign women, as well as the daughter of Pharaoh, women of the Moabites, Ammonites, Edomites, Sidonians, and Hittites from the nation of whom the Lord had said to the children of Israel, you shall not intermarry with them nor they with you, surely they will turn away your hearts after other Gods. Solomon clung to these in love. And he had seven*

Finding what God has placed in you!

hundred wives, princesses and 300 concubines and his wives turned his heart away. For it was so when Solomon was old, that his wives turned his heart after other gods and his heart was not loyal to the Lord his God. God had appeared to Solomon twice, once at Gibeon **1 Kings 3:5** next at Jerusalem **1 Kings 9:2** so the Bible doesn't say the spirit of God was in him but clearly he had a relationship with God but his wives did not. So, what was the foundation of these relationships? He must have been looking at the physical outward appearance, so he could not have found what God had placed in them. Because they had no relationship with God, they were not God's children.

When we think about finding what God has placed in you (being spiritually connected), many pastors, preachers, and teachers have not experienced this. How can a man of God that's being used by God to proclaim the gospel of Jesus Christ all over the world and his wife is not growing spiritually? I'm not saying she has to be leading other women of God, but she should be maturing spiritually and be finding the gift or gifts God has placed in her. It's all for God's glory.

All believers in Christ Jesus should be spiritually connected to someone that can help us grow and find our gift or gifts. Your pastor preaches or teaches on Sunday and Wednesday. That's not enough. You need a relationship with a brother or sister that can pour into you what God has poured into them! Praise God! This is why this book is vital to the believer. If pastors and teachers of the church don't have this and are not teaching this, the church will never get this knowledge!

www.ingramcontent.com/pod-product-compliance
Lightning Source LLC
Chambersburg PA
CBHW071036080526
44587CB00015B/2641